100% sales rule

100% sales rule

Jasmin Hajro

Jasmin Hajro

© 2020 Jasmin Hajro

All rights reserved

Written by Jasmin Hajro

Translated by Jasmin Hajro

Edited by Jasmin Hajro

Cover design by

Jasmin Hajro

First edition 2020

Hello,

yes 4.99 or 9.99 euries

you know that's euros right?

If you immediately start to complain,

, then you shouldn't read any further....

Life is not perfect,

we humans are not perfect ...

and we make mistakes and errors ...

First the price?

You can buy the "Hobbit" Story for 4.99 or 9.99

You can also buy the story about the clown IT

for 4.99 or 9.99.

After reading those stories you have nothing

I don't mean they aren't good stories,

they are fantastic....

But then you just have nothing

And the intention is that you will be left with a lot

after reading my book.

Why ?

Tips, action steps, strategy, tactics,

that get you results ...

I think you want to double your income,

your sales, your profits and your bank balance ...

If the price was a barrier for you, then hopefully you have passed over it, otherwise you should not continue to read this book ...

My company used to be a one-man business Hajro,

I was the owner,

I started it on September 1, 2015 ...

It sells greeting cards offline, door to door,

sets of 5 greeting cards.

On December 3, 2019, I founded Hajro BV,

at the notary,

on December 4 it was registered with the Chamber of Commerce.

It's the same business, different legal form.

It sells greeting cards,

gift mugs,

in this case coffee mugs filled with candy,

books and the like....

The like... is my author merchandise,

printed T shirts with slogans from my books.

It only sells books that I have written ...

The subsidiary is Hajro Publishing,

so that I pay less tax on the earnings from my book sales ...

Maybe you should first read what's on my author's website....

You can find it on

www.jasminhajro6.webnode.nl

There you can also download a bundle of mine for free ...

my first 10 books translated into english ...

I will also summarize it for you here,

so we can move on ...

I have published my books with many self-publishing companies such as Kobo.com,

Lulu.com,

Amazon.com at their KDP

the Kindle Direct Publishing,

at Streetlib.com,

draft2digital.com

and mijnmanagementboek.nl

I am an author and my own publisher ...

They offer self-publishing ...

So they only put your book for sale in their webshop.

You have to do the promotion and marketing and everything else yourself.

When people buy your book in their webshop, then they pay you your royalties properly .

That's 70% or less of the selling price ...

I also approached traditional publishers ...

One of their websites said the following:

Most books are written by ghostwriters …

It says that literally

and that publisher also offers that service….

Well….

Most authors are experts at something …

often at the subject of their book….

What does it tell you what it said…. ?

What does that tell you about most experts ?????

They haven't even written their own book, someone else did, so they have no expertise….

They are fake….

More actors than anything else….

I am ashamed to mention somewhere that I only

earn an average of E 500 per month ...

with my business ...

that's my monthly average this year

the year 2020 ...

And that I had only sold 500 books

of which paid and free titles....

But not anymore....

That's how it goes in reality ...

with a real company and a real author

I have written,

and improved all my books myself

I made my own covers,

translated into English myself

and self-published myself

because I am my own publisher, .

Nowadays my company Hajro BV is my publisher

because that is tax technically more advantageous.

Therefore, many of those "authors" "

not available by email, mail or telephone....

I think they do it for the following 2 reasons ...

Oh by the way when they say I don't have time to write ...

Bullshit ...

So you work 16 hours a day and 7 days a week, so you only have time to sleep and work and don't have 1 hour off every Sunday to write ???

Who lives like that?

You see it's bullshit and lies ...

They do it because....

1. It's easier

2. It is better if an experienced writer or copywriter writes the book, then it is much more likely that the book will sell well and they can make money off it.

Makes it harder for us, doesn't it?

Makes it more difficult for you,

as a reader

to choose the advice of real writers and real entrepreneurs ...

And it makes it harder for me as a writer

to gain your trust,

to build a relationship of trust,

so that you buy a book from me

and do what it says

and positively change your life or your business ...

Don't you think ?

Now I have to explain to you that I am real,

have real customers

and a real company ...

You can find Hajro BV at www.kvk.nl

That tells you that it exists,

is real and pays taxes.

That's the Dutch Chamber of Commerce by the way.

You can find the rest of the information on our

company website at www.hajro.be

You will soon notice that we do not have a physical store or an online webshop.

We have a company website,

and we sell products to consumers,

through house to house sales, direct selling, aka door to door sales

. Everything is aimed at direct sales.

Because after 5 years, I only had 2 orders,

while I have sold thousands of sets of greeting cards offline.

Why should I spend time on a web store or on a blog….

Maybe you have already learned some things here….

Did you also write them down?

Are you a serious student?

Or what …..

So on my author website, my 2nd ...

my first I paid too late and it went offline,

so I made a second one,

what I told you about

the www.jasminhajro6.webnode.nl

Make a note of it in your notebook ...

I call myself a writer because

I have written flyers, folders, brochures

, websites and books....

I am also an author,

of course a true author of more than 45 booklets ...

Yeah wow,

I am productive….

I have many and high goals

and I want to be able to take care of my family …

so I do more than average …

If you have written or are going to write a book

if you need a website….

Save yourself 65 or 100 euros per year

and create one for Free at www.webnode.nl

You also get such a long website name….

But that's the only drawback

for the rest it works fine

it is easy to make

and most importantly

it is online 24/7, 365

24 hours a day, 7 days a week, 365 days a year

You can have a website for yourself,

as an author or entrepreneur or expert in something

and one for your business, for your company….

I mainly position myself against fake "experts" "

on my author site.

By the way, this will be a short book …

Can you stand that?

Pay 9.99 for maybe 20 pages at most?

Can you handle it ?

I believe so...

Because you don't come to me for a fantastic hobbit story ...

but for practical ttips, right?

And that's one with 2 t's ...

Nothing to worry about ...

However ?

Or am I not that professional?

Oh my God....

Maybe a lot of professionals are fake too....

I will briefly introduce myself,

you can also read my biography on my author website, what I suggested you do first.

I am Jasmin Hajro, born in Sarajevo, Bosnia on July 6, 1985. We fled to the Netherlands when I was 10 years old.

I did the last part of primary school and then mavo and have a mavo diploma.

Which was of little use to me later when I was looking for work.

I've had several jobs often production work through employment agencies.

The longest I have worked for Landal Greenparcs, 4.5 years, first as a dishwasher, then as a cook.

I Started my first company 0-17 December 2012,

failed because I knew little about sales and marketing.

After that….Got an opportunity to sell greeting cards

on behalf of a foundation, received sales training….

when those people broke up I founded my own

foundation, the Giveth Life foundation.

Couldn't sell greeting cards full-time with that,

And I started my 2nd company, sole proprietorship

Hajro on September 1, 2015,

I kept selling greeting card sets,

years later my company is Hajro BV

and has shares or stocks ..

I am the Dga or

director major shareholder

and just like 5 years ago I am responsible for

everything.

You can find it on www.hajro.be

I worked about 6 to 7 days a week,

selling the house to house ... (door to door)

in the city of Doetinchem, Gaanderen, Wehl, Terborg,

Didam and surrounding places ...

After 1 year of working every week ...

Yes 1 year,

every week

plus 10 booklets

I got exhausted

and now I always rest on Sundays

and I also take Saturday and Wednesday off

if necessary ...

On average I gross that embarrassing E 500, - euros

per month ...

My BV pays much less tax than a sole proprietorship ...

Another thing for your notes ...

Invest 400 to 500 euros in a bv.

Similar to an LLC

Set it up at the notary,

you can go where i've been ...

026 Notarial office in Arnhem ...

In the long run, it will save you thousands of dollars

in tax.

Because there are so many fake "experts" "

I'm not as ashamed of my numbers as before ...

I am going through a normal development ...

As Brian Tracy says: "It takes 7 years to master a skill"

That's selling in my case

and then direct sales with the customer in front of me in person.

If you think: I can learn little from you because of your turnover.

Then you should go and read something else ...

But I hope you have learned that much of it

comes from fake experts and from professors and other theorists

who have no experience in selling or doing business.

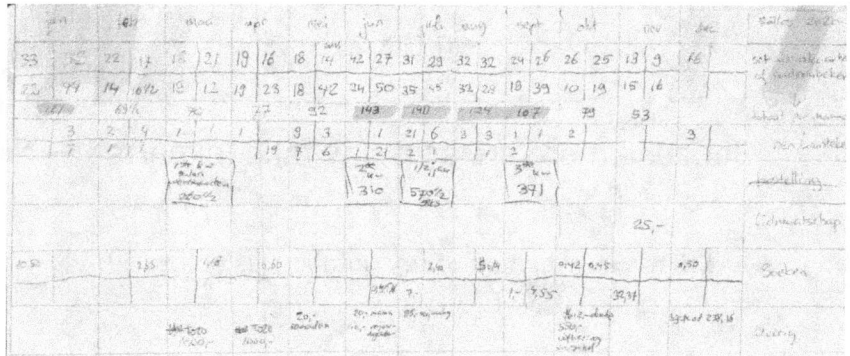

Those are my sales of my mugs, greeting cards and books

As you can see, I sell every week of the year and make sales evry week of the year.

... I've also had some support from the government, because of corona ...

Real numbers ...

who would show something like that?

Good

I doubled my sales in 2017

2017 Jul 23 sales

2017 Aug 32.5 sales

2017 Sept 43.5 sales

2017 Oct 18 sales

2017 Nov 86

November was my best month ever ...

I doubled my sales in 2018

2018 Jul 12 sales

2018 Aug 52.5 sales

2018 Sept 103 sales

My best month ever in September 2018

I doubled my sales in 2019

2019 Sept 59.5 sales

2019 Oct 86 sales

2019 Nov 130 sales

New personal best in November 2019

I have doubled my sales in 2020

2020 Mar 70 sales

2020 apr 77 sales

2020 May 92 sales

2020 Jun 143 sales

New personal best in June this year

My average monthly turnover in 2019 was E 282.79

My average monthly turnover in 2020 is E 500, -

That's almost double ...

I mainly did that by focus on the core activities.

That is with me:

selling greeting cards, mugs and pens....

Home to home , door to door...

Book sales are mainly done online

Dan S. Kennedy says, "Every business is the same "

So what applies to my company applies also for your company, in terms of sales and marketing ...

As you have also read on my author website,

my stuff is not for the lazy people...

people who are only willing to do 1 thing

to do.... 1 step,

while 5 or 10 steps are needed

If you are too, find something else to read,

hoping to read only will get you results....

The workbook also begins here I learned this

exercise from Brian Tracy and you are going

to do it.

I.

Also order this book as a paperback at
www.Lulu.com

or www.Mijnmanagementboek.nl

so that you can immediately write

your notes in it,

your ideas and

you can always read it back,

like every month.

II

Think of 20 ways to boost your sales

to increase.

Answer the question 20 times:

How do I make more sales?

1. I double the time that I am selling face to face with prospective people.

2. I do implement this tactic so that more people buy.
Get the promotion : buy 1 get 1 for free.

3. I read one book at least every month book about selling, preferably every week

4. I work 6 days a week,
I also sell every Saturday

5

6

7

8

9

10

11

12

13

14

15

16

17

18

19

20

21

22

You fill in the rest and WILL DO IT

Take every step

You want results, right?

Do the exercise and do every step.

III

Focus on selling it is the most important thing in your work life as a salesperson

And the most important thing in your work life as an entrepreneur or business owner.

Hell yes.

1. Forget TV,
2. forget social media,
3. check your mail once a month
4. check your email once a week or once quickly per day
5. Read about selling every day
6. Listen daily to audiobooks and seminars and webinars about selling or doing business (a lot you can find on youtube.com)

Learn to create multiple incomes for yourself…

1. Write down stories on www.medium.com

and sign up for their partner pro gramme,

so you get paid as people write your stories

2 write books and publish them to self publishers, as I have done.

3 Make sales in the morning,

create sales in the afternoon,

make sales in the evening

Also try to make sales on your spare day and

when you sleep ...

Seriously, when it's night with us and you sleep,

then it is day on the other side of the world ...

Hello

Hello

Opportunity ...

Hello

4. Do the exercise, answer 20 times the question,

How do I create 20 different ones incomes?

Do the exercise And after that ...

TAKE THE STEPS ...

Make it happen....

You've probably heard it before or read ......

I do not care because you are going to read it again ...

''Invest in yourself! ''

Ask yourself....

The year is almost over ...

How many books on sales do you have read this year?

How many books about sales do you already have firmly ordered for next year?

Think ahead..

Double the number of books that you order to invest in yourself

They can all be about selling and communication

go …

Get started !

Take the step!

If you don't book read

a month or week about sales,

get the book and slap yourself with it

You also learn from pain ...

Step 5 or something ….

Sell 100% of your working time!

Do you work 8 hours a day,

then only sell 8 hours a day,

nothing else

You also need to spend time

on adminis tration or marketing,

then there will be

a % of it of time on top of yourself

100% of your time selling

So selling 8 hours a day,

and after that

you read it well and understand it well ???

but will you also do it ?

So sell 100% of your time for 8 or 9 hours

a day,

then after that

you spend half an hour on your administration

or tax matters

or promotion

or studying your profession.

If you've come this far ...

Congratulations,

you really want to get better in selling,

or sales as we sometimes say…

I appreciate that ,

please remember the 100% sales rule

Do you remember how that goes?

It concerns your sales, your business and your life and changing the content of your wallet….!

Hell yes…

But first one more thing:

YOU MUST ABIDE THE 100% SALES RULE !!!

Every day 6 or 7 days a week

Become an www.Amazon.com affiliate and put some of their links from good selling products on your web site….

Can yield you some extra money right?

After you have 100% of your working time spent on sales,

then study marketing for 1 hour per day….

Then you are working 9 hours a day

So what ?

''Time will pass anyway''….

But one thing is certain,

you don't have to wait for anymore money,

because you will earn a lot more.

After you have 100% of your working time

spent on selling, and then 1 hour of marketing,

then spend 1 hour learning copy writing ...

Then you're working 10 hours a day ...

Well and time will pass anyway

But one thing is certain:

you're sales and bank balance are doubling and then again….

Lots of steps you've read now

wich explain the enormous success of

a few and the failure of many ...

Because many,

or most,

are only willing to take one step.

"At the time of translation, friday 11 december 2020….

BONUS :

If you abide by this 100% sales rule, you are selling 8 hours a day and 40 hours a week.

Are you ready ?

Here comes

The 200% Sales Rule

You start selling 7 days a week for 11,5 hours a day, that's 80,5 hours a week…….

I know it's madness…..

But you will double your sales in the first week, many times over….

And this rule is worth 100 times what you paid for this book…probably more…

Just do it
for a couple of weeks & transform your life.

The Ultimate Winning Strategy,

for salespeople & business owners

how to triple your sales & profits

In this powerfull book you'll discover :

The bio of entrepreneur & author Jasmin Hajro

&

The Ultimate Winning Strategy
for entrepreneurs

&

As a bonus : 4 previews

&

Plus a Bonus book :
Double your profits, extended

I sell sets of greetingcards and giftmugs door to door
in city Doetinchem and town Didam in the
Netherlands.
By now I am in business for myself
for 4 years. (Before this I had my forst business for about 3 years,
investment firm Jasko)
My business is called establishment Hajro and
you can find it at www.hajro.be
We also donate to 40 charities.
And it has many subsidiaries, you
can see them at :

My results in june 2018 : 15,5 sales (door2door)
1 membership sale 35,- euros in bookroyalties
my results in july 2018 : 12 sales (door2door)
my results in august 2018 : 52,5 (door2door)
45,- euros in bookroyalties
my results in september 2018 : 103 sales (door2door) 37,-
euros in bookroyalties.

The first thing you should learn from these numbers is to persist, no matter what.

The second thing you should learn from these numbers, is that I have tripled my sales & profits and that you can do the same.

By spending most of my time on selling, marketing, follow up and writing more books

That is what this book is about...

You can also find me at :
www.jasminhajro6.webnode.nl

The bio of author Jasmin Hajro, nice to meet you

Hello dear reader, how are you ?

Thank you for buying one of my books.

My name is Jasmin Hajro,
I was born on July 6, 1985 in Bosnia.
As refugees, we came to the Netherlands 21 years ago.
After having completed school & worked at several jobs ...

On 17 December 2012, I founded my first company: investment firm Jasko. After a successful first year, I unfortunately had to close that company.

After a short period of rest, unemployment and temporary work.
I started again as an entrepreneur.

On September 1, 2015, I founded establishment Hajro.

(We say establishment instead of company, because
we do a bit more then just sell stuff.
Like providing jobs, donating
to 40 different charities,
and helping people to live richer.)

Since the beginning the core activity is,
selling sets of greeting cards, door
to door.
Nowadays the product range has been expanded.

With, among other things, the selling of my 12 books.

The royalties of my books are donated to the charity: foundation
Giveth Life.
From there more than 40 other charities receive
donations.
And by buying this book, so do you. Thank
you.

My company is now part of Hajro Group,

which consists of 19 different subsidiaries,
that are part of 1 umbrella organization. Called
Energy Now (Energie Nu)

For more information about my company
& the foundation, go to www.hajrobv.nl

" By the way, I started my first company in 2012. I

have made more than 700 sales since

1 September 2015 so far.

So I have a track record in
sales and business,
and I know what I'm talking about. "

"" As you have probably already understood,
I earn my money by selling for my own company.
That's my work.

The proceeds from my books go to charity.

I write from experience,
I write to help people move forward in
their lives and business "

The Ultimate Winning Strategy for entrepreneurs

How do we measure success in business?
With monetary points, with earned euro's or dollars.

What is a successful business?

Successful entrepreneurship = selling
a lot

We are therefore successfully running our business, if we sell a lot.

So success in doing business = selling a lot
(many sales realized / many sales closed)

Because sales means profits.

So what is the Ultimate Winning Strategy in business?

First we start with the concept, then you get 2 examples from real life

Have you noticed that supermarkets are open 7 days a week?

Supermarkets may be a less good example, because we just have to eat and drink.

Have you been to the Esso gas station? (Part of Exxon mobil corporation) The Esso gas station has a shop with staff, and is open 24 hours a day, 7 days a week.

And no, even if it seems that we need petrol, the Esso could also have become a self-service gas station, where you fill your tank and pay with a creditcard.

But the Esso has a shop with staff, 24/7 .

What do the supermarkets do every day?

<u>They make sales and profits.</u>
<u>Every day !</u>

What does the Esso do every day and night?

The Esso makes sales day and night,

every day.
<u>So the Esso makes profits, every</u>
<u>day and night of the year</u>

The supermarkets and the Esso are successful because
they realize sales every day
and thus make profits every day.

The Ultimate Winning Strategy for entrepreneurs is

making profits every day.

Make a profit every day of the year.

You do that by selling every day, and
by daily closing sales.

Your advantage over your competition

If you sell every day & make profits every day, do you than have an advantage over companies who only make profits 5 days a week?

Example 1 from real life

I have been selling from Monday, September 18, 2017 untill
Wednesday, September 27, 2017,
10 days in a row, and made
22 sales in total.

So every day I made sales & I made profits everyday.

That is the Ultimate Winning Strategy for entrepreneurs in
action.
(in the real life of running your business)

Well if we are honest, then we know that
the transaction value of sets of greeting
cards is modest.
And therefore the profit per sale is also.

But do not be turned off by those numbers ... You will soon
receive a real life example from someone who made 1 million.

This was to make you understand the successful Concept
of the Ultimate Winning Strategy for entrepreneurs and
that you see proven that it works.

You now understand that Concept, you have
seen some examples of companies
applying the Ultimate Winning Strategy.
You have seen a real life example from me I
have proven to you that it works.

And you are 100% assured that the Ultimate Winning Strategy
works.

People do not need greeting cards
like they need food and drinks, but
they bought every day and I made
profits every day.

So it does not matter what kind of product or service you sell.

<u>The Ultimate Winning Strategy also works for you.</u>

<u>Next step</u>

You understand the Ultimate Winning Strategy for
entrepreneurs,
and you know it works.

So now you are going to do it.

You are going to implement it.

I'm not asking you to work 7 days a week, although
you should do it once.
(That will boost your confidence)

You can sell from Monday to Friday & hire
someone who sells for you
from Saturday to Monday (a part-timer)

Then you will already have sales every
day and profits every day.

If I can do it alone, then you can certainly
do it with 2 people!

Are there any other ways how you can make sales everyday & profits ever day?

Consider, think and find 20 ways, with which you can make sales everyday and therefore make profits everyday.

Write them down.

1 Hire a salesperson
2 Create a team of salespeople
3
4
5
6
7
8
9
10 11
12
13
14
15
16
17
18
19
20

Example 2 from real life

Go to www.youtube.nl and
watch the video of Walter Bergeron, GKIC
marketer of the year.

The video lasts about half an hour.

Pay close attention when he says: that means also on saturdays
and sundays.

(that he was selling 7 days a week and making
profits every day)

Have you seen
what the Ultimate Winning Strategy for entrepreneurs can
do for you?
Go to work,
go out selling every day & making profits every day.

Apply your 20 ways, give
your sales a boost, make
lots of profits.
Every day of the year.

I wish you a lot of succes.

Remember as you apply the

Ultimate Winning Strategy,

that the McDonalds is open 7 days a week

and they make sales and profits everyday…

they are very succesfull

as you already know,

now you know their strategy…

Met vriendelijke groet,

Jasmin Hajro

Hajro bv

Unieke wenskaarten,
cadeaugeschenken & boeken

KvK : 76564770

www.hajro.be

Author website :

www.lulu.com/spotlight/jasminhajro

P.S. If you have liked this book and got good value from it,
than would you be so kind
to recommend it to people that you know.
So that it also helps them forward.
Thank you.

I would like to give you another book as a gift

It's called Recipe for Happiness, and
it can help you achieve your sales and
businessgoals.

Beacuse If you are more relaxed and happy, you
will be more productive

You can read it on the following pages.

Enjoy.

The Recipe for Happiness

A book has been written about a true story ...
About a man who was imprisoned in a
concentration camp at the time of Hitler, and
happy.

So, Happiness has nothing to do with your circumstances.
It has everything to do with, your
choice to be happy,
regardless of circumstances.

Choose to be happy.

Of course there are touhger times in life, like
when someone you love, dies.
That's part of life.
Those times of grief you just have to go through and process.

Processing is best done by talking about it, to
get it off your chest regularly.

Or by writing about it,
if you write down a situation or your feelings about it, then
it's on paper,
and it is less in your head.

Writing is a good outlet.

Processing is also done well by: staying busy.
Whether that is in your work or your hobby.
They say: a rolling stone does not collect moss. So
stay busy ....

Okay, now you have learned a good lesson about how to better process negative life experiences.

But you're here for the Recipe for Happiness, right?

Well, the lesson you've learned will help to make the recipe work better for you.

Here it comes then …

You have probably read a local newspaper, and you regularly check the news.
(the daily news on television)

Have you noticed that about 99% of it is bad news?
Only misery .. If you
did not know better,
you would think that the whole world is going to perish.

If it's a habit for you,
to watch the news every day for half an hour …

Have you ever wondered if it's healthy for you?
Does it make you happy ? Of
course not !

The easiest way to change a habit is by replacing it with a new habit.

So from today on, instead of watching the worldly news half an hour a day ……….

Watch COMEDY for half an hour a day.

Mandatory.

Every day.

Well, now at half past eight in the evening it's not news time, but Comedy time.

If you watch comedy, you relax & you laugh. Sounds healthier, doesn't it?

Well, laughing every day is easy to do, right?

And replacing your old bad habit in this way, with a nice, healthy new habit, is probably easier than you thought.

Except for the fact that relaxation is good for you, when you laugh, also your body makes endorphins. Those are natural happiness substances.

Well, after 21 days of daily watching comedy, you will have formed a new habit.

So watch Comedy every day.

You can watch a lot of standup comedy on Youtube for free.
Simple?
Sure, but you
have to do it, every
day,
until you don't have to think about it anymore, and you start doing it automatically.

Some Happiness Ingredients in a row:

- Watch comedy every day, at least one hour.
- Eat ice cream, treat someone with an ice cream.
- Work out, throw out your frustration by playing tennis or go for a run.
- Pee in the yard (and if you get a fine for urinating, laugh your ass off)
- Do not worry, life is too short for that (by staying busy, you do not have time to worry) – Hug the people that you love
- Go enjoy a cup of coffee or tea
- Buy or save a cat or some other pet
- When you receive money, immediately save a part of it
- Don't let the media scare you, the world is not getting worse, the world is getting better.
- Sex, need I say more (when you have sex your body also
- produces endorphins = those natural happiness substances)

Maybe the Recipe for Happiness is different than you had expected....

But that doesn't matter, the
point is that it works &
that it will help you to live happier.

Do it, it is easier
then looking with a sour face.
If you liked this book & got some value from it.
Would you then be so kind, please,
to recommend it to the people
that you know.
So that they too can enjoy it and
live happier.
Thank you very much.

It was my pleasure to write and translate this book
(my third one) for you.
I hope it helps you to live happier.
(I know it will, if you do the things it teaches)

And I hope, that we can together make a contribution to
more happiness in the world.
We can.
If you recommend this book and share it.
Then I will promote it.
And together we will make a contribution to a
happier world.

I would appreciate it if you would write a short review.
Thank you for your effort.
Kind regards,
Jasmin Hajro

(old business card
do you like the new one ?)

Preview book Build your fortune

the Pay yourself first principle

It means that when you receive your money, you first pay yourself, by for example, setting aside a tenth.
To clarify your result, we will make an example calculation.

For example, you earn 3000 euros or dollars per month. And you pay yourself first, in other words: you put aside a tenth (10%) of your income. So you save 300, - euros per month.

A year has 12 months,
So after 1 year you'll have (12 x 300) = 3600, - euros.
After 1 year you have put a whole month's salary aside.

If you put aside a tenth every month, how much will you have after 10 years? (3600 x 10) = 36000, - euro.

So after 10 years you have 36000 euros or a whole year's salary in your saving account.

Later on in this book: Build your Fortune, you'll see how to make that amount that you put aside each month.
Grow faster.

Preview book Build your Fortune

10% of everything

It is important that when you first pay yourself, by setting aside 10%.
That you put 10% of everything aside.

Of course 10% of your income.

But also 10% of the tips if you receive any, also 10% of your surtax, also 10% of the money you receive as a gift, also 10% of your 13th month, also 10% of your bonus, also 10% of your wage increase, also 10% of your tax refund, also 10% of your welcome bonus, also 10% of your holidaypay.

No matter from which angle or from whom you receive money, the first thing you do with it, is to pay yourself first.
By setting aside a tenth of it.

End of preview.

Preview book Moneymaker

Moneymaker 3

The bible for entrepreneurs, written by an entrepreneur. So your daily reading.
No, it's not about GOD.
It says, written by an entrepreneur .....
YOU READ ONLY BOOKS WHICH ARE WRITTEN BY PEOPLE WHO HAVE THEIR OWN COMPANY !!
Do you understand ?

This way you prevent feeding your mind with BULLSHIT.
And that you will model BULLSHIT. So
you save yourself time and money.

Ok, then a bit about that Entrepreneurial Bible.
It is called No Excuses, the Power of self discipline
And is written by Brian Tracy
And yes, he has his own company.

Otherwise his name would not be here.

It comes down to self discipline.
And self discipline makes you feel very good about yourself.
When you exercise, for example, while most people watch TV.
When you work on a Saturday, while most people have a weekend. When you take a step towards achieving your goals on Sunday.

The above 3 examples require discipline from you.
But 1, 3, 5 years from now where
will you wind up ?
And where will most people wind up ?

Have you ever worked a day with pain because your teeth were broken?
Have you ever worked with only 2 hours of sleep, the night before?
Have you ever worked without having slept the night before?

It was probably easier to watch TV then .....
But if I did, then I would be a Bullshitter for you, and not someone who you respect.
I disciplined myself and went to work.

Oh yeah, buy the entrepreneurial bible.
NOW.

Previeuw book Moneymaker

Moneymaker 2.

Two things that you have to spend your time on daily Which 2 are they?
Watch TV and be on Facebook?

Without B.S., so:
SALES & DIRECT MARKETING
If you sell something (sales), then profit comes in.
If you become good at (direct marketing), then profit comes in.
With marketing you save yourself time while selling. You do not have to explain who you are and what your company does during your presentation.

How many hours per working day do you spend on sales?
How many hours per working day do You spend on Direct Marketing?

WHAT HAPPENS IF YOU ONLY SPEND YOUR WORKINGTIME ON SALES & DIRECT MARKETING ??

Will you have more profits and therefore more money?

End of preview
For more information about this book by me, go to
www.jasminhajro6.webnode.nl

Small introduction with establishment Hajro

Establishment Hajro is committed to helping the people in the province of Gelderland,
by providing jobs and keeping people working,
by donating to more than 15 Charities, and by helping people to live richer.

Today Hajro is a subsidiary of Hajro Group.
The Hajro Group consists of Hajro International,

Hajro Publishing, Hajro Consulting and Hajro Franchise among others

We now have several products & services, and we support more than 15 charities that really help people.

Visit us at **www.hajro.be**

and discover what more we can do for you.

Hopefully you will become a raving fan & customer of us.
However you choose,
I wish you a lot of prosperity &
happiness.
Kind regards,
Jasmin Hajro

Met vriendelijke groet,

Jasmin Hajro

Hajro bv

Unieke wenskaarten,
cadeaugeschenken & boeken

KvK : 76564770

www.hajro.be

Author website :

www.lulu.com/spotlight/jasminhajro

old card

book Would you like more success in door to door selling ?

Perhaps the shortest book in the history of selling books? With a.o. → answer to how to sell more with door to door direct sales .. -> why small profits are good and how you can easily add them to what you are selling now → how you perform better by relaxing more → where you will find a unique opportunity to start an affordable franchise with a good reputation of the company with unique products of which you can easily sell many because you have experience with selling house to house → advice crashed, the principle remains the same P.S. If you are lazy and are not going to do anything about this book, or think that just reading it will magically change your life. Then you don't have to read it! Hello my name is Jasmin Hajro on September 1, 2015 I started my one-man business Hajro, which sells sets of greeting cards and donates to charities. On December 3, 2019 I turned it into a BV, I then founded Hajro BV. That sells greeting cards, gift gifts and books online and offline & donates to 40 Charities. Our website is www.hajro.be By offline I mean selling house to house ... I've been doing that for over 5 years, it gives me satisfaction and money. I like to do it... Of course there have been days when I didn't feel like it, when I was tired, too tired, too exhausted, a bit sick and felt miserable ... Often I still went to work ... I was not advised to give advice in my books about entrepreneurship, because of my turnover at the time ... We are now going to trash that advice ... Because the principle remains the same ... So whether I earn 100 in a month selling house to house Or that I earn 600 euros in a month selling house to house Or that I earn 1200 euros by selling house to house ... The principle remains the same. The 5 steps & the 8 steps. You know them. You learned them in your sales training. There were also some other reasons for the low turnover ... I was robbed, tagged and drugged ... Shit happens ... But that might be material for another book .. I do recommend buying cameras and putting them in your house. When people smell money, they come and get it in nasty ways ... like by drugging you ... Anyway here some figures ... 2019 Jan 51 sales, 14 pen sales = 269, - Feb 77 sales, 4 pen sales plus 35, - book royalties = 424, - Mar 54 sales, 5 pen sales = 275, - Apr 33 sales = 165, - May 33 sales, book royalties 34.46, side job 367.63 in total = 567.09 Jun 2 sales, side job 733.94 in total = 743.94 Jul 2 sales, side job 1313.12 in total = 1323.12 Aug 22 sales = 160, - Sept 59.5 sales = 297.50 Oct 86 sales, 2 pen sales, 1 member subscription worth 22.50, side job, book royalties 20, - = 504.50 Nov 130 sales, 12 pen sales = 662, - Dec 81 sales, 12 pen sales = 417, -

---

2020 Jan 121 sales, 10 pen sales plus 10.50 book royalties = 625.50 So you can see that I went from 33 sales in April 2019 to 130 sales in December 2019. The principle remains the same. At the time, I just focused a bit more on selling house to house and spent more time house to house with prospects and customers. But the principle remains the same. even though I earned 4x more .. Same city, same people, same products, same prices ... The 5 steps and the 8 steps. The principle remains the same. That's what I learned from my coaching sessions ... 1 focus on my core business (selling greeting cards and gift cups, door to door) 2 innovate, give people more choice (I then designed different designs of greeting cards for birthdays) But I will only say it once, the principle remained the same even though I earned 4 times more selling house to house And 3 small profits are good (because if a number of customers no longer buy from you, you don't feel that way, because they are only euros) Have you found some wisdom yet? Or do you find the short book disappointing and not worth 2.99 euros .. It can save you thousands of euros ... that which you have just read .. If you are also going to DO it. And by the way, the revelation: you can earn a good income with small profits You see with 8 to 9 sales per day ... even if every customer pays you only 5, - then you already have a normal income per month.

```
1 pld x 30 dagen = 150 p/-
2 sales pld x 30 dagen = 300
3 sales pld x 30 dagen = 450
4 sales pld x 30 dagen = 600
5 sales pld x 30 dagen = 750
6 sales pld x 30 dagen = 900
7 sales pld x 30 dagen = 1050
8 sales pld x 30 dagen = 1200
9 sales pld x 30 dagen = 1350
10 sales pld x 30 dagen = 1500
11 sales pld x 30 dagen = 1650
12 sales pld x 30 dagen = 1800
13 sales pld x 30 dagen = 1950
14 sales pld x 30 dagen = 2100
15 sales pld x 30 dagen = 2250
```

You can also see from the schedule ... that if you start selling a few hours on Saturday and a few hours on Sunday, it will pile up at the end of the month ... You can put your weekend earnings on your Fortune account ... You can live on your weekday earnings. And by the way.... You can rest after some sales 5 customers on Saturday and you are free ... all day for you ... 5 customers on Sunday and you are free for the rest of the day ... But still nicely put E 50, - euro on your Fortune account. And still be able to rest and do fun things. That is much better. You've probably also been taught not to behave like most people in your sales training ... So selling a few hours on Saturday and selling for a few hours on Sunday, putting some money in your Fortune account every weekend and you have an edge over most people ... also write down your goals and study your sales profession and you will go to the top of society and the people. So you sell more with door to door sales: → if you focus on selling every day → if you persevere when you don't feel like it and it is difficult → if you offer people different variations of your product → when you build relationships, so that you get regular customers, by staying in touch with those people → if you work according to my schedule → if you spend more time house to house presenting to prospects and customers → if you also sell a number of hours on Saturday and Sunday → if you save money and can invest in, for example, a printed pen, which you then sell for 1 euro each, because small profits are good → if you leave a flyer or folder with interested parties, like a pro (don't deliver but leave it behind) -> if you continue to learn and study your profession → if you jerk off or finger before you go to work, because then you are more relaxed → if you jog or exercise that makes you sweat, because after that you are happier and more relaxed and therefore more effective in selling and persevering and persevering. -> if you always persist, no matter what the fuck happens

That's how I went from 33 sales to 130 sales ... and that's how I will go from 130 sales to 260 sales ... The principle remains the same and hopefully you will sell more house to house thanks to my advice from this bundle ... I once made 10 sales in 1 day, and 1 x 14 sales in 1 day ... 2 of my good days ... I know I can & I also know that You Can I wish you a lot of succes

Remember : only application of what you have learned
only doing the things you have learned
only taking action
gets you results !

Hopefully you'll become a praising customer of mine.
A raving fan..
I wish for you a lot of happiness, health and piles of money.

More books by Jasmin Hajro :

Build Your Fortune

Moneymaker

Recipe For Happiness

the Lifebuoy For Banks "Loyal Banking"

the Ultimate Winning Strategy, for entrepreneurs

(which is for salespeople & businessowners too)

Poems, jokes and book

Victory 1

Victory 2

Always employment & always money in your pocket, everyday.

Things You Don't Want To Know.

Challenges in having your own business, in real life.

how to Grow your money & Build a good retirement in 2 hours per month, for moms, dads, career women and busy people .

Overcoming tough times.

Secrets of writing and selling books.

Double your profits.

Double your profits, extended.

Triumph 1 (boxset)

Triumph 2 (boxset)

Victorious series (boxset)

Through the crisis

Victory 3

My story

My little masterpiece

Victory 4

I don't feel like writing, says the author

Hackers are scouts

Being real and true: in times of fake and pretend

Lifechanging quotes

the Jasmin Hajro lifestory (which includes Victory 1,2,3,4)

Controversial

This is how you get rich: passively

Please visit my author website at
www.jasminhajro6.webnode.nl

I give away 10 free books.

And you can find my services
and become an affiliate or writer of articles
and earn by working with me.

Be so kind to rate this great book on sales
from real life experience
with 5 stars
and a good review,
just say why others should read it.

Thank you.

www.ingramcontent.com/pod-product-compliance
Lightning Source LLC
Chambersburg PA
CBHW07043422O526
45466CB00004B/1672